Seven Wonders of
TRANSPORTATION

Ron Fridell

TWENTY-FIRST CENTURY BOOKS
Minneapolis

To my mother and father

Twenty-First Century Books
A division of Lerner Publishing Group, Inc.
241 First Avenue North
Minneapolis, MN 55401 U.S.A.

Website address: www.lernerbooks.com

Library of Congress Cataloging-in-Publication Data

Fridell, Ron.
     Seven wonders of transportation / by Ron Fridell.
         p.   cm. — (Seven wonders)
     Includes bibliographical references and index.
     ISBN 978–0–7613–4238–0 (lib. bdg. : alk. paper)
     1. Transportation engineering—Juvenile literature. I. Title.
  TA1149.F75 2010
  629.04—dc22   2009020318

Manufactured in the United States of America
1 – DP – 12/15/09

Contents

INTRODUCTION

*P*EOPLE LOVE TO MAKE LISTS OF THE BIGGEST AND THE BEST. ALMOST TWENTY-FIVE HUNDRED YEARS AGO, A GREEK WRITER NAMED HERODOTUS MADE A LIST OF THE MOST AWESOME THINGS EVER BUILT BY PEOPLE. THE LIST INCLUDED BUILDINGS, STATUES, AND OTHER OBJECTS THAT WERE LARGE, WONDROUS, AND IMPRESSIVE. LATER, OTHER WRITERS ADDED NEW ITEMS TO THE LIST. WRITERS EVENTUALLY AGREED ON A FINAL LIST. IT WAS CALLED THE SEVEN WONDERS OF THE ANCIENT WORLD.

The list became so famous that people began imitating it. They made other lists of wonders. They listed the Seven Wonders of the Modern World and the Seven Wonders of the Middle Ages. People even made lists of undersea wonders.

GOING PLACES AND DOING THINGS

This book is about Seven Wonders of Transportation. Transportation is the movement of people and things from place to place. Transportation has two parts. The first part of transportation is vehicles, such as cars and trucks. The second part is infrastructure, such as roads, highways, railways, and bridges. Infrastructure helps vehicles move smoothly and quickly to places near and far.

Transportation helps people go places and do things. People take buses and ride bicycles to school. They drive cars and ride subway trains to work. Transportation also helps move things from place to place. Any item you buy in a store probably came by truck over the highway. Some items traveled even farther by rail, sea, or air.

Our basic need for transportation hasn't changed over the years. But transportation technology, or tools, has changed. Long ago, people relied on muscles and wind to power vehicles. For instance, strong animals pulled carts. Winds pushed sailing ships. As inventors discovered better power sources, people created new kinds of vehicles. The first motor vehicles were steam powered. Then gasoline engines replaced steam engines. In the twenty-first century, people have started to use a cleaner energy source to power cars. That source is electricity. Electric cars could soon be a common sight on U.S. roads. We can't say for sure what the future will bring. But we can be sure that vehicles will continue to improve.

A WONDERFUL JOURNEY

Transportation brings changes. Highways help people visit distant places. Subway lines open hidden worlds beneath a city's surface. Transportation also brings excitement. Giant cruise ships carry thousands of tourists to fascinating new lands. Spacecraft fly people to the moon. This book will take you on a journey as well. It will show you Seven Wonders of Transportation that have changed people's lives.

On your journey, you will see these seven wonders come to life and grow. You will see how a few dirt paths grew into a vast series of trade routes that spanned continents. You will learn how people designed and built a transportation system unlike anything ever seen before. You will follow two brilliant brothers who showed the world that people could fly. These and other wonders await you. Turn the page to begin your journey.

Commercial air travel is one of the modern wonders of transportation.

1 THE *Silk Road*

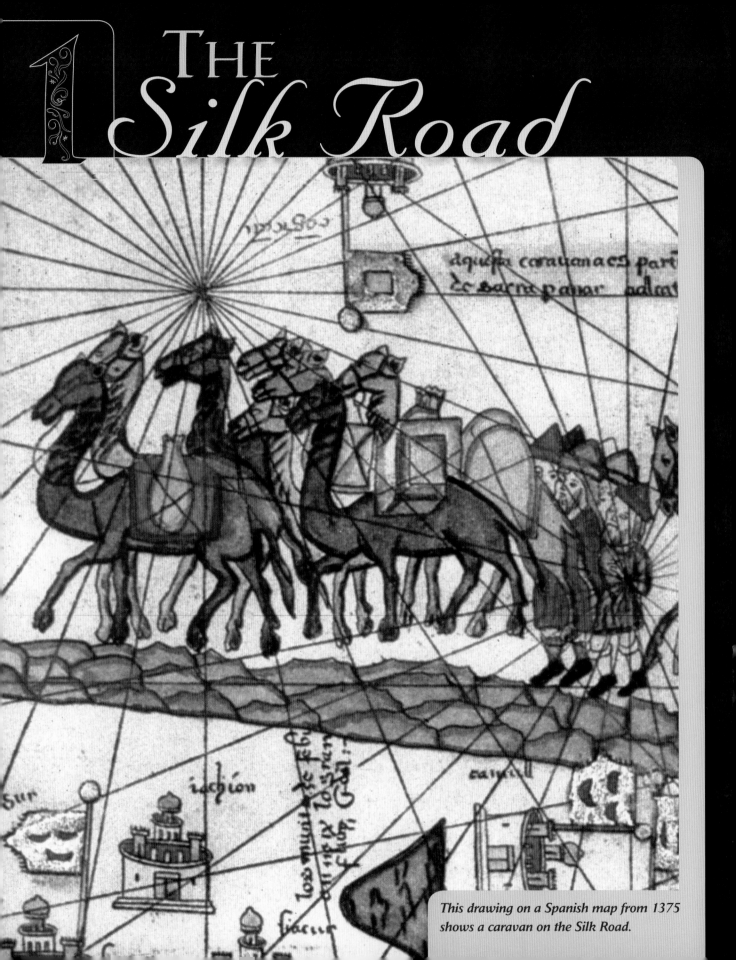

This drawing on a Spanish map from 1375 shows a caravan on the Silk Road.

*A*LL THROUGH HUMAN HISTORY, PEOPLE

HAVE NEEDED ROADS FOR TRANSPORTATION. IN ANCIENT TIMES,

TRADERS, EXPLORERS, AND OTHER LONG-DISTANCE TRAVELERS

NEEDED PATHWAYS TO GUIDE THEM.

The first roads were simple dirt paths from one village to another.
People traveled over the paths on foot. Animals pulled carts along the
paths. Over time, the roads grew wider and longer.

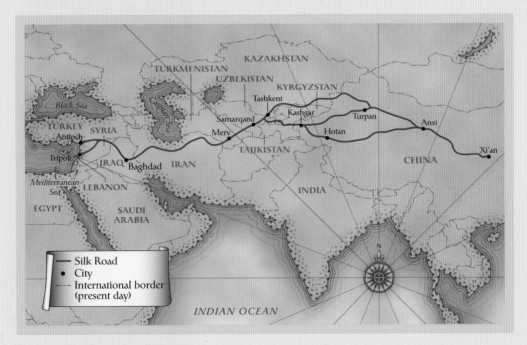

People also built roads to faraway places. Workers cut and cleared brush. They rolled aside boulders and dragged away trees. They built bridges over rivers. Workers also connected roads running in different directions to make road networks. People built forts, inns, religious centers, and other buildings along the roads. Eventually, the groups of buildings turned into villages and cities.

The most famous ancient road network was the Silk Road. About twenty-five hundred years ago, people began using the Silk Road to travel between China and the Middle East. People used this wonder of transportation for nearly ten centuries.

GOODS AND IDEAS

The Silk Road wasn't a single road. This "road" was actually a series of separate east-west routes. The main Silk Road passed through China and central Asia, including modern-day Uzbekistan and Turkmenistan. It continued on through modern-day Iran, Iraq, Lebanon, and Turkey. Side routes passed through modern-day India, Indonesia, Saudi Arabia, and Egypt. These rugged routes guided travelers across rough seas, hot deserts, and mountain passes.

Traders from Asia journeyed west along the Silk Road in search of items they could not get close to home. They bought silver from Spain, perfumes from Greece, ivory and ostrich eggs from Africa, cinnamon and pepper from India, and other precious goods. Traders from Europe, Africa, and the Middle East journeyed east along the Silk Road. They bought tea, spices, ceramics, paper, playing cards, jade, cloth, and other items from China. The traders resold these items to customers in their home countries. Goods purchased from Silk Road traders came from exotic worlds that the customers had never seen.

EVER Wonder?

How did the Silk Road get its name? The most precious item traded on the ancient Silk Road was Chinese silk. In the West, silk was as precious as gold.

Silk comes from silkworms. When they are young, these insects spin coverings called cocoons. Cocoons are made of silk fibers. The coverings protect young silkworms as they grow into adults. On silk farms, people raise silkworms for their cocoons. Workers collect the silk fibers. They twist the fibers together to make silk thread. They weave the thread into silk cloth.

Some travelers still cross the Taklimakan Desert of western China in camel caravans, just as travelers did during the Silk Road era.

But goods were not all that traveled east and west along the Silk Road. News and ideas also made the journey. People from East and West got together in inns and other resting places. They shared languages, religions, cultures, recipes, games, poetry, and news. Before the Silk Road, the peoples of Europe, the Middle East, Africa, and Asia were strangers to one another. The road introduced them.

WU TI AND THE HEAVENLY HORSES

The Silk Road's long, colorful history is alive with tales of bold adventure. Many stories tell of Chinese emperor Wu Ti. He took the throne at the age of sixteen. This ambitious and powerful ruler helped spread the Silk Road's fame through China and beyond.

Wu Ti ruled from 140 to 87 B.C. When he came to power, China had little contact with the rest of the world. Wu Ti changed that. He sent teams of soldiers and government officials westward along the Silk Road. He ordered them to bring back news of the outside world.

The expeditions brought reports of strange and fascinating peoples and places along the Silk Road. One piece of news in particular caught Wu Ti's attention. He learned about a breed of big, fast horses 2,000 miles (3,218 kilometers) to the west. Warrior people in central Asia raised these horses for their size and speed. They were faster and fiercer in battle than all other horses.

Wu Ti had to see the horses for himself. He ordered his armies to bring some of them back to China. But the central Asians who bred the horses refused to part with them. Wu Ti's armies had to fight two wars to capture the animals. In 102 B.C., Wu Ti's armies brought one thousand of these extraordinary animals back to their emperor. Wu Ti was pleased. The horses gave his armies new speed and power. The Chinese called the horses *tian ma*, which means "heavenly horses."

This sixth-century Chinese image shows Emperor Wu Ti with two government officials.

CELEBRATING *Horses*

More than one thousand years ago, Chinese poet Tu Fu wrote about Wu Ti's heavenly horses. He wrote:

> Lean in build, like the point of a
>   lance;
> Two ears sharp as bamboo pikes;
> Four hoofs light as though born
>   of the wind.
> Heading away across the endless
>   spaces,
> Truly, you may entrust him with
>   your life.

THE TRAVELS OF MARCO POLO

Marco Polo was the Silk Road's most famous European traveler. He was born in Venice, Italy, in 1254. Marco's father and uncle were merchants. In the 1260s, they traveled to China along the Silk Road. They returned to Venice and planned another trip to China. This time they took Marco with them. In 1274 the travelers reached the palace of Kublai Khan, the Chinese ruler.

Marco Polo was an expert storyteller. He delighted the khan with enchanting tales of life in Italy and his travels along the Silk Road. Kublai Khan insisted that Marco stay in China, and Marco did. For seventeen years, he traveled throughout China. He traveled to places that no European had seen before.

Marco Polo was also a writer. He filled journals with detailed notes of his travels. Later, he turned his notes into a book about his adventures along the Silk Road. This book, *The Travels of Marco Polo*, was hugely popular in Europe. Like the Silk Road itself, the book helped introduce West and East.

Marco Polo is introduced to Kublai Khan. Polo's father and uncle are dressed as friars (men of the church) in this manuscript painting from Jean de Mandeville's Book of Marvels, *which dates from the fourteenth century.*

INVASION OF THE ARCHAEOLOGISTS

The Silk Road was the major trade route between West and East for centuries. After about 1350, traders used it less and less. One reason was sailing ships. European traders started traveling to Asia by sea. Carrying goods by ship was faster and easier than carrying them over land.

Warfare also played a part. China's rulers feared invasions from Mongolian warriors to the north and west. The Silk Road gave these powerful enemy armies direct paths to and through China. So China's rulers shut down trade along China's part of the Silk Road.

The Silk Road was quiet for the next five hundred years. Then, in the 1800s, archaeologists invaded. These scientists study the remains of ancient civilizations. Archaeologists learned about the ruins of ancient cities along China's portion of the Silk Road. Paintings, manuscripts, and other ancient treasures were there for the taking. Archaeologists from Europe, Russia, and Japan came to find them. They shipped ancient Silk Road treasures to museums around the world.

China no longer allows foreign archaeologists to haul away its treasures. Instead, Chinese archaeologists uncover them. Museums in China display them. Modern-day tourists can visit stops on the Silk Road and see many of the ancient treasures.

LOST IN THE *Desert*

No European knew more about life along the Silk Road than Marco Polo. In one journal entry, he explained how travelers kept themselves from getting lost in the vast deserts of central Asia. He wrote, "Before they go to sleep they set up a sign pointing in the direction in which they have to travel." Travelers also had to keep track of their animals. "Round the necks of all their beasts they fasten little bells, so that by listening to the sound they may prevent them from straying off the path," Marco Polo wrote.

"I have only told half of what I saw, because no one would have believed me."

—*Marco Polo on his deathbed, 1324*

Left: *Archaeologists excavate a house in a Silk Road city near the Caspian Sea.* Right: *This Chinese silk damask, a firm fabric, is from the sixth century. Silk from China was a precious trading commodity carried from East to West.*

TOURISTS ON THE ROAD

At the Silk Road city of Xi'an, China, visitors can see a display called the "Terra Cotta Warriors and Horses." This is a collection of more than eight thousand life-size ceramic warriors, horses, and war chariots. Chinese craftspeople created the figures about two thousand years ago. After the Chinese emperor died, workers placed the ceramic figures in his tomb. The figures were arranged in columns, as though they were preparing for battle. They were supposed to protect the emperor in the afterlife.

In modern times, people can visit the emperor's tomb and see the figures on display. Each figure remains in the exact spot where it was first placed two thousand years ago. Modern workers have built a giant dome to cover the tomb. The dome protects the figures from the weather. Other workers are still uncovering figures at the site. They repair damaged figures in the site's "hospital" area.

How were the terra cotta warriors and horses discovered? Archaeologists are not the only people who find ancient treasures. In 1974 some Chinese farmers were digging a well. To their amazement, they uncovered some of the statues.

Archaeologists have uncovered thousands of terra cotta soldiers and horses buried in a tomb along the Silk Road.

A family shops at the Sunday market in Kashgar, China. Buyers can find all kinds of household goods and foods at the weekly bazaar there.

The ancient city of Kashgar, China, is another Silk Road attraction. Kashgar sat at the intersection of two Silk Road routes. This location made it an important trading center. People came there to buy everything from spices and wool to cattle and knives. Modern Kashgar is still an important trading city. At its colorful Sunday market, merchants sell spices, food, clothing, and much more.

Samarqand, Uzbekistan, is another ancient Silk Road city. It was an important stopping point for traders and travelers. Modern visitors to the area can still see ancient caravansaries. Traders rested at these inns at night. In Xi'an, Kashgar, Samarqand, and other cities along the way, the East-meets-West spirit of the ancient Silk Road lives on.

"The precious merchandise of many foreign countries is stored up here. The soil is rich and productive, and yields abundant harvests."

—Xuanzang, a Chinese traveler, describing Samarqand, A.D. 646

2 THE *Bicycle*

Cyclists crowd the course during stage 6 of the 2009 Tour de France. The Tour de France is one of the most famous bicycle races in the world.

$\mathcal{T}$HE WHEEL IS A WONDER OF TRANSPORTATION.
BEFORE THIS ROUND, ROLLING MARVEL WAS INVENTED, PEOPLE
HAD TO USE MUSCLE POWER TO TRANSPORT CARGO ON LAND. TO
MOVE THINGS OVER SNOW AND ICE, PEOPLE LOADED CARGO ONTO
SLEDS. HORSES, REINDEER, OR DOGS PROVIDED THE PULLING POWER.
ANIMALS ALSO CARRIED LOADS ON THEIR BACKS. SOMETIMES ANIMALS
DRAGGED LOADS OVER BARE GROUND. BUT DRAGGING THINGS ON
THE GROUND CREATES FRICTION. FRICTION IS THE RUBBING OF ONE
THING AGAINST ANOTHER. FRICTION SLOWS MOVEMENT.

This European figurine from the fifteenth century B.C. is an early example of wheels as transportation.

With the invention of the wheel, people said good-bye to all that friction. Rolling is the secret. A wheel rolls around a center bar called an axle. Together, the wheel and axle made transporting people and cargo a whole lot easier and faster.

People in the ancient Middle East were the first ones to use wheels. The invention appeared there more than five thousand years ago. Wheels arrived in Europe later on, about thirty-four hundred years ago. No one knows whether the wheel came to Europe from the Middle East or whether a European reinvented it.

In the twenty-first century, wheels of all sorts and sizes roll all over the world. Think about shopping carts, wheelbarrows, roller skates, skateboards, scooters, tractors, trailers, motorcycles, automobiles, trucks, and trains. All these vehicles depend upon wheels. They couldn't operate without them. The same goes for the world's most widely used vehicle, the bicycle.

WHEELS, WHEELS, *Everywhere*

Wheels aren't just for transportation. Wheels allow drawers to slide in and slide out. The disk drive in a computer is a wheel. So are the pulleys in cranes and the gears in clocks. And let's not forget giant amusement park rides called Ferris wheels. From huge to tiny, wheels set all sorts of things in motion.

EARLY BICYCLES

Bicycles take the wheel and connect it directly to human muscle power. The rider pushes down on pedals. The pedals turn a crank. A chain connects the crank to the bicycle's rear wheel. The harder the rider pedals, the faster the bicycle moves.

You wouldn't expect a vehicle to arrive on the scene in finished form. The bicycle was no exception. It took a while to grow up. The first bicycle appeared in 1817 in Paris, France. People called it the hobby horse.

At first glance, the hobby horse looked a lot like a modern bicycle. It had two metal wheels connected by a wooden or metal frame. At second glance, the differences stand out. The hobby horse had no pedals, crank, or chain. Riders did not sit on it. Instead, they straddled the frame and pushed the machine along with their feet.

> *"On the avenues, people ride on a vehicle with only two wheels, which is held together by a pipe. They sit above this pipe and push forward with movements of their feet, thus keeping the vehicle moving."*
>
> —*Chinese official describing bicycles in Europe, 1860s*

A Wonder Grows Up

A new kind of bicycle appeared in the 1860s. People called it a boneshaker. The name was painfully on target. The bicycle's metal wheels and iron tires made for a bone-shaking ride. This bike had wooden pedals attached directly to the front wheel. It had no chain to move the back wheel. This front-wheel drive made for a hard, slow ride over the cobblestone streets of the day.

The man at left is riding a hobby horse. The man at right is pedaling a boneshaker. This photograph was taken in the mid-nineteenth century.

In 1870 the high-wheeler arrived on the scene. Its front wheel was 53 inches (135 centimeters) wide. That's more than twice the size of a typical modern bicycle wheel. With its huge front wheel and tiny back one, the high-wheeler was a fascinating sight. It had solid rubber tires—a big improvement over metal. But the high-wheeler was tricky to ride. It was dangerous too. Swerving suddenly or braking hard could propel the rider high over the handlebars and headfirst to the ground. Only the young and fearless dared ride a high-wheeler.

The modern-style bicycle finally arrived in 1885 in Great Britain. Called the Rover Safety Bicycle, this bike had pedals set between the wheels and a chain attached to the rear wheel. Rear-wheel drive transformed bicycles from toys into useful long-distance vehicles. In the late 1880s, bicycle makers added air-filled rubber tires for a more comfortable ride. The bicycle had grown up.

WOMEN AND CHILDREN NEXT

Bike riding has always been fun. But at first, it wasn't for everyone. Before the 1890s, men did all the riding. Bicycle makers didn't manufacture bikes for children. And back then, riding a bike was a men-only activity. Many people thought that sports and exercise were unladylike.

This men-only attitude started to change in the 1890s. That's when women began riding bicycles. This new activity required new, more comfortable clothing.

"She who succeeds in gaining the mastery of the bicycle will gain the mastery of life."

—*Frances E. Willard, women's rights leader, 1895*

For riding bicycles, many women wore bloomers, or baggy pants, beneath their skirts. Some men objected. They said that women shouldn't wear pants. But women stood their ground. They loved having the freedom to exercise in light, comfortable clothing. They also loved being able to travel on their own.

The bicycle helped make women freer and more independent. Susan B. Anthony was a pioneer for women's rights. In 1896 she stated that the bicycle had done more for women's freedom than anything else in the world.

Young people wanted to enjoy the fun and freedom of bicycles too. But for a long time, bikes were made only in adult sizes. That changed in the late 1910s. Bike makers started to make kid-size bicycles. It wasn't long before young people everywhere were zooming along on bicycles built especially for them.

EVER *Wonder?*

How popular can one bicycle get? One model of kids' bike set all-time sales records. It was the Schwinn Sting-Ray *(below)*. With its banana seat and high-rise handlebars, it looked like a low-slung motorcycle called a chopper. In 1968, 70 percent of all bikes sold in the United States were Sting-Rays or Sting-Ray copies.

A SURGE OF BICYCLES

In the twentieth century, bicycles surged in popularity. One reason was technology. Bikes became lighter, easier to ride, and safer. Bike makers used lightweight aluminum to make wheels, handlebars, and seat posts. Special gears made pedaling up hills easier. Hand-operated cable brakes made slowing and stopping safer.

Variety was another reason for the surge. Bicycle makers produced different kinds of bikes that appealed to different kinds of people. Some manufacturers made tandems, or bicycles built for two—and sometimes three, four, and more. On a tandem, two riders sit one behind the other. The front rider steers, and both riders push the pedals. Other bike makers made unicycles. These one-wheeled bicycles have pedals and a seat, but no handlebars. Acrobats ride unicycles in circuses, but ordinary people ride them too.

In the 1970s, manufacturers introduced two bold new styles: BMX bikes and mountain bikes. They appealed to young people looking for competition and adventure. BMX is short for bicycle motocross. BMX racers pedal furiously around a dirt track. They skid around corners and jump over bumps and dirt ramps. They wear helmets, kneepads, and elbow pads for protection. BMX bikes feature lightweight frames. They have wide, knobby tires that absorb shocks.

Like BMX bikes, mountain bikes are made for rugged riding. Mountain bikers ride on forest roads, dirt paths, and mountain slopes. They make their way up and down steep inclines. That's why a mountain bike might have eighteen, twenty-one, or even twenty-seven different gears. With low gears, a cyclist can pedal up steep hills and even mountain slopes without struggling and straining. High gears are for cruising down steep hills.

THE SURGE CONTINUES

In the twenty-first century, bicycles are more popular than ever. In fact, worldwide, bicycles outnumber gas-powered vehicles by more than two to one. In countries such as China, where many people can't afford cars, people use bicycles to go to and from work. Often, rush-hour traffic in China has more bicycles than cars. Even in wealthy countries such as France and Japan, many people use bikes instead of cars to get to work and run errands.

Commuters in crowded cities such as Shanghai, China (right), *often ride bicycles to work rather than drive cars.*

EARTH-FRIENDLY
Bicycles

Bicycles are good for the environment. Motorized vehicles pollute the air with exhaust fumes. This pollution contributes to global warming, or rising temperatures on Earth. Motorless bicycles don't pollute at all.

Professional cyclist Lance Armstrong tests a new racing bicycle in a wind tunnel in 2008.

Money is one big reason for all the bikes in the world. A bicycle costs far less to own and operate than a motorcycle, car, or truck. Bikes are also more energy efficient than motorized vehicles. The only fuel they burn is human energy—muscle power.

Modern bikes are lighter and stronger than earlier versions. In the 1950s, an average road bike weighed about 65 pounds (29 kilograms). In the 2000s, the typical bike weighs half that much. Racing bikes weigh only about 20 pounds (9 kg) at most. To make bikes lightweight, designers use metals and materials such as titanium, carbon fiber, and Kevlar. These are the same materials used to make airplanes and spacecraft. They are superlight and superstrong.

Lighter materials make modern bikes faster. So does aerodynamic, or streamlined, design. Aerodynamics is the study of how air flows around objects. To make bikes more streamlined, designers use a structure called a wind tunnel. Inside the tunnel, wind from a giant fan blows past a bicycle and a dummy rider bolted to the seat. Machines measure how easily the wind moves past the bicycle. The more quickly and smoothly the air moves, the faster the bike can go. Designers keep making changes to build bikes with the greatest possible speed. The world's most widely used vehicle keeps getting better and better.

3 THE LONDON Underground

The subway in London, England, known as the Underground, transports more than three million passengers each day.

$\mathcal{W}$HAT DO PEOPLE DO WHEN BIG-CITY STREETS GET DANGEROUSLY OVERCROWDED? WHERE DO THEY GO WHEN THE STREETS CAN NO LONGER HOLD ALL THE VEHICLES AND PEOPLE ON FOOT?

Residents battle for space on a London street in the 1820s.

They go underground. They build a subway—a transit system that runs from station to station beneath the city's surface. Riders enter stations at street level and go underground on stairs, elevators, or escalators. At the bottom are tunnels with train tracks. When a train arrives, doors slide open for riders to board and take seats. If the seats are full, passengers must stand in aisles. They hold onto poles and to straps hanging from the ceiling. As the train stops at each station, more riders get on. Others get off and make their way back up to street level.

More than 160 cities have subway systems. Among them are New York and Boston in the United States; London, England, and Paris, France, in Europe; and Shanghai, China, and Bangkok, Thailand, in Asia.

OVERCROWDED LONDON

The world's first subway system was built about 150 years ago in London. In the mid-1800s, London suffered badly from overcrowding. Cars had not yet been invented. But tens of thousands of wagons and carriages pulled by tens of thousands of horses filled the streets.

To handle this growing problem, workers built an aboveground, steam-powered train system around central London. Six railway stations ringed the city. The train system helped reduce foot and horse traffic in central London, but the streets were still too crowded. By the 1850s, London's transportation problems had hit the breaking point. There was no room to expand the aboveground railroad. What then?

FEARS AND DOUBTS

The British government announced a bold new proposal. It would build an

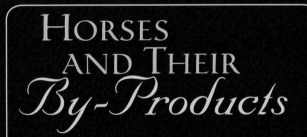

HORSES AND THEIR *By-Products*

In crowded central London during the 1800s, horse manure made a big mess. According to one estimate, the city's horses produced 100 tons (90 metric tons) of the foul-smelling stuff each day. And much of it remained on the city's streets. Workers known as crossing sweepers made a living from the problem. People who needed to cross a street could pay a sweeper to walk ahead and brush the manure aside to clear a path.

underground railway tunnel beneath the inner city. This system would connect all six aboveground stations. Each passenger could exit the train at the station closest to his or her downtown destination.

This radical plan made some people nervous. The idea of huge machines rumbling along beneath their feet led to dark thoughts. What if the steam trains shook nearby houses, cracking walls and breaking windows? What if fumes from the engines poisoned passengers? What if the fumes came up through cracks in the ground and poisoned people on the street? What if the weight of the street traffic above caused the tunnels below to collapse?

Joseph Paxton was a famous British architect of the time. He doubted that anyone would use trains that ran beneath the city's surface. "People, I find, will . . . never go under ground; they always like to keep as much as possible in the ordinary course in which they have been going," he said.

This drawing shows the plan for the Baker Street Station during the development of the London Underground.

"I should think these Underground railways must soon be discontinued, for they are a menace to health."

—London Underground passenger, 1887

He thought riding a subway would be a big change and people do not like change. The subway also posed physical problems. The project was vast. The expense would be enormous. The dangers of construction were many. Worst of all, no one could say for sure that an underground railway would really work. London would be the very first city in the world to attempt to construct one.

CUT AND COVER

Despite these doubts and fears, construction on the London Underground began in 1860. Workers used a method called cut and cover. Construction crews cut down through surface streets. They dug trenches 15 feet (4.6 meters) deep for the train tunnels and rails. They walled up the sides of the trenches with bricks and roofed them over with brick and iron supports. Finally, workers rebuilt the streets above.

It was not an easy job. Gasoline-powered trucks, cranes, and bulldozers had not yet been invented. London's thousands of subway workers had only picks and shovels to dig with. They did most of the work by hand.

On opening day, January 10, 1863, nearly forty thousand eager passengers proved Joseph Paxton wrong. They took a ride on the London Underground Circle Line. A few months later, the Underground was carrying more than twenty-six thousand passengers every day.

BRIDGES *Underground*

You never know what you'll run into when you dig deep beneath the surface. The Paris subway system opened in 1900. Construction crews who dug down to build it met with some surprises. They tunneled their way into several huge, open underground spaces. Some were ancient burial vaults full of human bones. In some places, workers had to build bridges across the caverns to hold the subway track. If you ride the Paris subway, you'll travel across some truly unique structures: underground bridges.

Above: *Politicians and engineers in London tour the world's first underground line in May 1862.*
Below: *The first underground train passes beneath Praed Street in London in 1863.*

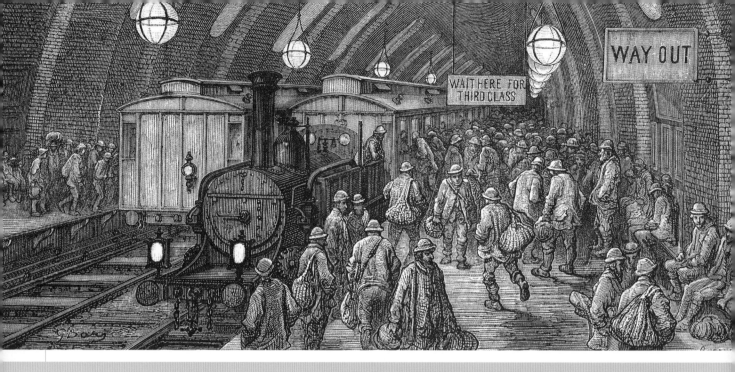

This engraving by Gustave Doré shows a busy underground station in late nineteenth-century London.

ELECTRICITY TO THE RESCUE

Not all passengers enjoyed the ride. The steam locomotives were noisy. To make the steam to drive the engines, workers stoked train furnaces with tons of coal. Air pollution was an unhealthy by-product. The air in the train cars filled with choking coal dust and sulfur.

Electricity eventually solved the noise and pollution problems. In 1882 in New York City, U.S. inventor Thomas Edison switched on the world's first electrical power system. By 1905 the London Underground was ready to go electric too.

DEEP-LEVEL AIR-RAID *Shelters*

During World War II (1939–1945), German planes bombed the city of London. The bombings were frequent and heavy. So the city turned eight subway stations into air-raid shelters to protect citizens from bombs. Workers dug tunnels and caverns beneath each station. The shelters had bathrooms, medical stations, food storage rooms, air vents, and thousands of bunks.

When German bombers approached, air-raid sirens sounded a warning. Londoners then streamed down spiral staircases into the shelters. Sometimes they stayed for only a few hours. Sometimes they stayed much longer. Sirens sounded again when the raid was over. Then everyone would return to street level.

British citizens took refuge in London's underground tunnels during wartime bombings by the German air force in 1940.

Quiet electric train cars replaced the roaring locomotives. All that coal dust and sulfur vanished too. The London Underground became the first subway line to operate electric trains.

THE TUBE

Through the twentieth century, the Underground kept right on growing. New routes ran beneath the central city and out to suburbs to the north, south, east, and west. Workers used a new, improved method to construct them.

With the old cut-and-cover method, workers had dug up entire city streets to make tunnels. With the new method, they did not cut into the streets. Instead, they dug a wide entrance hole deep into the ground. From there, they hollowed out tunnels beneath the surface. Gasoline-powered machines burrowed through dirt and rock. The project left surface streets fully intact. The method was called deep-level tube tunneling. That's why Londoners refer to the Underground as the Tube.

In the twenty-first century, the London Underground has 253 miles (407 km) of track connecting 268 stations. It is the longest public transportation system in the world. Each year more than one billion passengers ride the Tube's more than four thousand subway cars. Without this wonder of transportation, London would not be London.

TERROR AND *Safety*

On an ordinary day on the London Underground, accidents and injuries are rare. But July 7, 2005, was not an ordinary day. That morning, a small group of terrorists set off bombs in London subway cars. Terrorists use fear and violence to promote a cause or movement. Public transportation systems are tempting targets for terrorists. The London subway bombers killed fifty-four passengers and injured hundreds more. The terrorists also bombed a bus.

Police shut down the entire subway system. They led a quarter million people out of train cars and tunnels to safety. By the next morning, most of the London Underground was again operating normally. Of the 20 people thought to be involved in the bombings, three were charged and brought to trial. They were acquitted in April 2009.

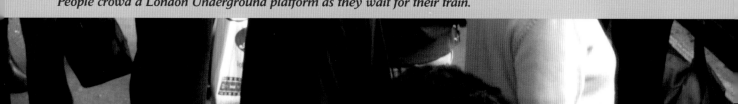

"To the gentleman wearing the long grey coat
trying to get on the second carriage, what part of
'stand clear of the doors' don't you understand?"

—London subway train public address announcer, 1999

People crowd a London Underground platform as they wait for their train.

4 FLYING Machines

In the early twentieth century, human flight became a reality instead of just a dream. Here a French aviator flies a plane in 1909.

$\mathcal{F}$LYING MACHINES MAY BE THE MOST WONDROUS OF ALL THE WONDERS OF TRANSPORTATION. FOR THOUSANDS OF YEARS, PEOPLE DREAMED OF FLYING. FOR HUNDREDS OF YEARS, THEY STRUGGLED TO MAKE THE DREAM OF HUMAN FLIGHT COME TRUE.

This model of a flying machine is based on drawings that Leonardo Da Vinci made in the late 1400s or early 1500s.

In earlier centuries, a few people tried flying like birds. They made machines with wings that flapped up and down. These wing-flapping contraptions all failed. But people learned from their mistakes. Yes, wings had to be part of a flying machine. But the wings could not flap. They had to be fixed firmly in place. Fixed wings on an airplane produce an upward force called lift. This force helps keep planes in the air.

This illustration shows Icarus falling into the sea after flying too close to the sun.

ANCIENT FLYING *Dreams*

People have imagined flying since ancient times. Two thousand years ago, the ancient Greeks told a story about human flight. In the story, a boy named Icarus wears a pair of wings made of feathers and held together by wax. He flaps his arms and flies high into the air. Flying makes Icarus feel powerful and proud. But this pride is his downfall. He flies too close to the sun. The wax melts, the feathers blow away, and down Icarus falls into the sea. The story is a cautionary tale, or warning. The moral: Flight is for the gods only. It is not for humans.

Wilbur Wright works in the Wright brothers' bicycle shop in Ohio in the late 1890s.

But lift was not enough. Flying machines needed power from an engine. In the late 1800s, people invented small, lightweight gasoline engines. At last, inventors had all the tools they needed to build flying machines. Two American brothers, Wilbur and Orville Wright, were the first inventors to make a successful, powered airplane flight.

A MATTER OF CONTROL

One key to the Wright brothers' success came from a surprising source: the bicycle. In 1892 the brothers opened a bicycle shop in their hometown of Dayton, Ohio. Bicycles were all over the U.S. roads at the time. More than three hundred U.S. companies built more than one million bikes a year.

At their shop, the Wright Cycle Exchange, the Wrights designed, built, and sold bicycles. Their business made a good profit. But they were more interested in flying machines. The brothers read newspaper stories about pilots who could not control their aircraft. The Wrights knew that if humans wanted to fly, they had to master their flying machines.

The Wrights' hands-on work with bicycles gave them confidence. The Wrights knew that balancing on a bicycle was tricky. They believed that if a rider could control a bicycle, then a pilot could control a plane. The brothers were determined to be the first to do it.

Flying Machines

37

BIRDS AND BIKE RIDERS

To control a plane, a pilot must master three forces: pitch, yaw, and roll. Pitch is the up-and-down movement of an airplane's nose. Yaw is the movement left and right.

Then there's roll. That's the tricky one. Roll is the rocking movement an airplane makes when one wing dips lower than the other. Cars do not roll. They stay level, because their tires run on solid ground. Planes, however, fly in an ocean of air. Pilots must control roll to one side or the other to keep airplanes balanced. If a pilot can't control roll, the aircraft might spin and dive. How did the Wrights master roll?

This is where bicycles came in—and birds too. The brothers noticed that birds

To design airplane wings, the Wright brothers studied the mechanics of birds in flight.

FLIES *and Spies*

When the Wright brothers copied birds in flight, they were using the science of biomechanics. *Bio* comes from the Greek word *bios*, or "life." Mechanics is the study of how things move. The Wright brothers looked at birds to see how they moved, as if they were looking at machines.

Modern inventors also use biomechanics. Some scientists used special slow-motion cameras to study how houseflies fly. The scientists used what they learned to build a robot that looks and moves like a fly. They hope to turn this "Robo-Fly" into a teeny-weeny spy equipped with a tiny camera and microphone.

in flight move like bike riders. They bank, or lean, into turns. Pilots needed to bank into turns too, the Wrights decided. When turning left, a pilot had to lower the plane's left wing a bit. When turning right, the pilot had to lower the right wing. Banking helps control roll and helps keep an airplane balanced.

WING WARPING

The brothers noticed something else about birds. As birds lean into a turn, they twist the tips of their wings. These twists help birds roll left or right. Could a pilot twist the wingtips of a plane and get the same results?

Wilbur Wright discovered how. He built wings made of cloth, wrapped around a wooden frame. The wingtips were flexible. Control wires in the airplane connected the wingtips to a pedal at the pilot's foot. When the pilot pushed the pedal, the wires pulled the wingtips, bending them. Wilbur Wright called his revolutionary new control system wing warping.

The combination of banking into turns and twisting wingtips helped give the Wrights the control they needed. But their airplanes still needed years of testing.

BUILD, TEST, REBUILD

In 1900 the Wrights began three years of designing, building, and testing aircraft. At home in Dayton, they built a wind tunnel to test wing shapes. To test the airplanes, they chose a beach in Kitty Hawk, North Carolina. This site had strong, steady winds to help planes stay aloft. It had wide, sandy dunes for soft landings and no trees to get in the way of airplanes. At the test site, the Wrights first built and flew gliders. Gliders are planes without motors.

In 1902 the Wrights tested a glider that flew better than anything they had tried before. From this test, they saw that they needed a bigger plane. In 1903 the brothers built a plane called the *Flyer*. It was taller, wider, and heavier than any plane they had built before. The *Flyer* was a biplane. It had two sets of wings, one on top of the other. The Wrights fastened a gasoline motor to the lower wing. Bicycle chains connected the motor to two wooden propellers at the back of the plane. The plane was ready to make history.

The Wrights tested their new plane at Kitty Hawk on December 17, 1903. The *Flyer* was the first powered aircraft to successfully fly under a pilot's control. It flew four times that day. Each brother piloted two flights. The longest flight lasted only fifty-nine seconds and covered just 850 feet (259 m). But this was long enough and far enough to make the age-old dream of human flight come true at last.

U.S. PATENT No. 821,393: *Flying-Machine*

A patent is a government document that explains how an invention works and gives legal rights to the inventor. The Wright brothers' patent for their flying machine explained their unique control system in detail. The plane was flown "with the operator lying face downward . . . with his head to the front, so that the operator's body rests on the cradle." From this cradle, or frame, the pilot used ropes, cables, pulleys, and pedals to control the plane's wings, nose, and tail. This system allowed the pilot to control the forces of pitch, yaw, and roll.

"[The brothers] shook hands, and we couldn't help notice how they held on to each other's hand . . . like two folks parting who weren't sure they'd ever see each other again."

—John T. Daniels, who helped launch the Flyer in 1903, recalling the first flight, 1927

Wilbur Wright runs alongside the Flyer as Orville Wright makes the first powered flight on December 17, 1903. The flight lasted only twelve seconds and covered 120 feet (37 m).

> *"Be it known that we, Orville Wright and Wilbur Wright . . . have invented certain new and useful Improvements in Flying-Machines."*
>
> —*Wright brothers, from their patent for a flying machine, 1903*

FROM NORTH CAROLINA TO OUTER SPACE

The Wrights' 1903 gasoline-powered biplane was the first of its kind. People used it as a model for more airplanes. Since 1903 people have built millions of planes. They include everything from single-seat ultralight airplanes to jumbo jets.

When did the dream of human flight extend from Earth to outer space? In 1865 French author Jules Verne published *From the Earth to the Moon.* In this science-fiction story, he tells of three men who build a spacecraft. They load it into a cannon and shoot themselves to the moon.

Verne was one of the first writers to imagine setting foot on another celestial body. On July 20, 1969, U.S. astronaut Neil Armstrong became the first person to actually do it. The *Apollo 11* spacecraft had taken Armstrong and two other astronauts to the moon. While one astronaut remained in the main spacecraft, a landing craft carried Armstrong and fellow astronaut Buzz Aldrin to the moon.

When Armstrong stepped onto the moon's surface, he said, "That's one small step for [a] man, one giant leap for mankind." And let's not forget who took the very first step: the Wright brothers on the sands of Kitty Hawk way back in 1903.

Astronaut Buzz Aldrin walks on the surface of the moon during the first moon landing on July 20, 1969.

The space shuttle Endeavour *prepares for takeoff in July 2009. In the near future, everyday citizens might be able to travel to space.*

FLYING INTO
the Future

What's next for flying machines? People have some far-out ideas. Some people envision tourist flights into outer space. The tourists would stay in space hotels.

Another idea is orbital passenger flight. Here's how it would work: spacecraft would orbit, or circle, the Earth continuously. They would fly at super-high speeds, just above the layer of air surrounding Earth. Shuttle planes would take passengers up to the orbiters. Once on board an orbiter, a passenger would speed around the world. Another shuttle would transport the passenger from the orbiter down to his or her destination on Earth. In this way, passengers could fly anyplace on Earth in ninety minutes or less.

5 THE *Interstate* HIGHWAY SYSTEM

Traffic flows on Interstate 81 in Middletown, Virginia.

$\mathcal{W}$HEN THE FIRST EUROPEAN SETTLERS SAILED TO NORTH AMERICA IN THE 1600S, THEY CAME TO A LAND WITH VERY FEW ROADS. MOST SETTLERS BUILT THEIR HOMES ALONG THE OCEAN OR RIVERS. THEY OFTEN TRAVELED FROM PLACE TO PLACE BY BOAT. TRAVELING BY LAND WAS DIFFICULT WITHOUT A SYSTEM OF ROADS.

Over the centuries, Americans gradually built roads across the continent. In the twenty-first century, the United States has nearly 4 million miles (6.4 million km) of roads. People can use these roads to travel just about anywhere in the nation.

One highway system links every major city in the lower forty-eight states. It crosses the country east to west, from Maine to California; and north to south, from the Canadian border to the Mexican border. It's the Dwight D. Eisenhower National System of Interstate and Defense Highways—better known as the Interstate Highway System (IHS). With more than 46,000 miles (74,000 km) of roads, eighty-two tunnels, and more than fifty-five thousand bridges, the IHS is the largest highway system in the world.

All IHS highways look a lot alike, because all are built to the same strict standards. The highways have no traffic lights, stop signs, or railroad crossings. All have at least four lanes, with at least two lanes traveling in each direction. A narrow strip of land called a median separates traffic going in opposite directions. Each lane is 12 feet (3.7 m) wide.

Since the days of the Silk Road, people have built roads to carry travelers, settlers, and goods. They have also built roads to move warriors, weapons, and military supplies. People built the IHS for the same reasons.

A WILD RIDE

The idea for the IHS began nearly a century ago. On July 7, 1919, a convoy of U.S. Army vehicles set out from Washington, D.C., bound for San Francisco, California. The eighty-one trucks, trailers, automobiles, and motorcycles were

EFFICIENT BUT *Boring*

Because all IHS roads are built alike, they look much the same all over the United States. The roads are safe and efficient. But driving on roads of the same size and design can be boring. TV news commentator Charles Kuralt had this to say about the IHS: "It is now possible to travel from coast to coast without seeing anything. From the Interstate, America is all steel guardrails and plastic signs, and every place looks and feels and sounds and smells like every other place."

packed with 297 soldiers and officers. The expedition was called the First Transcontinental Motor Convoy (FTMC).

The FTMC had two missions. One was to see how swiftly an army could travel across the continent in case of a military emergency. The other mission was to persuade the U.S. public that improving the nation's highways would be good for everyone.

The convoy traveled through eleven states. It followed a northern route along a road called the Lincoln Highway. One day this gravel road would become the world's first transcontinental (coast-to-coast) highway. But in 1919, it was far from complete. The convoy had to travel over muddy dirt roads, narrow mountain paths, and the shifting desert sands of Utah and Nevada.

Officers kept written records of the convoy's progress. Each day was a genuine adventure. Many of the soldiers behind the wheel had never driven a military vehicle before. Accidents were common. Cars and motorcycles skidded into muddy ditches. Trailers overturned. Trucks sank into quicksand. Bridges gave way.

After sixty-two days of hard traveling and more than 230 accidents, the soldiers and officers of the FTMC reached San Francisco. They had covered

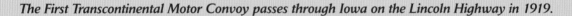
The First Transcontinental Motor Convoy passes through Iowa on the Lincoln Highway in 1919.

> *"The automobile won't get anywhere until it has good roads to run on."*
>
> —Carl G. Fisher, businessman and promoter of the Lincoln Highway, 1912

about 58 miles (93 km) per day for a total of 3,251 miles (5,230 km). The convoy's average speed was 6 miles (9.7 km) an hour.

A SUCCESSFUL JOURNEY

All along the way, crowds came out to greet the 2-mile-long (3.2 km) convoy. People had never seen anything like this mighty display of military vehicles. One of the FTMC officers was a young lieutenant colonel named Dwight D. Eisenhower. "The truck train was well received at all points along the route," he wrote. "It seemed that there was a great deal of sentiment for the improving of highways, and, from the standpoint of promoting this sentiment, the trip was an undoubted success."

People agreed with Lieutenant Colonel Eisenhower. The nation needed a well-maintained system of long-distance highways to deal with emergencies. For instance, people needed to travel quickly during fires, hurricanes, and other natural disasters. And the military needed good roads in wartime.

Building a long-distance highway system would help Americans in another way. At that time, most Americans lived east of the Mississippi River. It was difficult for people to live and do business in the West because the roads were so rough. A network of long-distance highways between the Mississippi River and the Pacific Ocean would bring more people and businesses to the West.

People agreed that the United States needed a national highway system. But it would cost billions of dollars. Government officials could not agree on how to pay for it. So, for a while, Americans talked about the system but did not build it.

IDEAS IN HIS HEAD

Meanwhile, the age of the motor car had arrived. In 1919 the Ford Motor Company alone produced one million automobiles. And Ford was just one of many car companies. Car owners were eager to hit the road and drive long distances. But, as the FTMC had learned, most of the nation's roads and highways were a mess, especially in the West.

People who loved automobiles couldn't wait. They formed the Good Roads Movement. The movement worked with state and local governments to pave existing roads and build new ones.

In the 1930s, the federal government got involved in road building. By then the United States was in the Great Depression (1929–1942). Millions of Americans were out of work. President Franklin Roosevelt created an economic program called the New Deal. As part of the New Deal, the government hired millions of workers for building projects. Some of the workers constructed roads and bridges.

The Good Roads Movement and the New Deal helped for a while. But road building came to a halt during World War II. The nation focused on winning the war instead of building roads. During that war, Dwight D. Eisenhower became a five-star general. He led all the troops of the United States and its allies fighting in Europe. From 1944 to 1945, he oversaw the defeat of Germany. This work gave Eisenhower a chance to take a good look at German roads.

What Eisenhower saw put ideas in his head. The German highway system, the autobahn, linked different regions of the nation. The broad, straight highways were all built to the same strict standards. Cars could travel long distances at high speeds without stopping. Military troops and supplies could move swiftly and efficiently. This is the kind of highway we need in the United States, General Eisenhower decided.

Germans travel down the autobahn in the mid-1930s. The German autobahn was Eisenhower's inspiration for the Interstate Highway System.

FROM START TO FINISH

After the war, Dwight D. Eisenhower served two terms as president of the United States. From the start, he pushed hard for a nationwide highway system. President Eisenhower convinced Congress to go along with his idea. In 1956 he signed into law the Federal Aid Highway Act. This act allowed the United States to build a national network of roads much like Germany's autobahn. The states would pay 10 percent of the cost. The federal government would pay the rest.

The original plan was for 42,000 miles (67,578 km) of highways. The first section of interstate opened in November 1956. It was an 8-mile (13

Highway construction and engineering supervisors celebrate the completion of the first 8 miles (13 km) of U.S. interstate near Topeka, Kansas, in 1956.

WHY HAWAII? Why Not Alaska?

Interstate highways link all the U.S. states except Hawaii and Alaska. Hawaii is not linked with any other state by road because it is an island state in the middle of the Pacific Ocean. But 50 miles (80 km) of Hawaii's highways are built to federal standards. So they are part of the IHS. None of Alaska's highways are built to federal standards, so Alaska's roads are not part of the IHS.

Interstate 105 in Calfornia was the last piece of the original Interstate Highway System to be finished.

km) stretch in Topeka, Kansas. The last link in this plan, Interstate 105 in Los Angeles, California, was completed thirty-seven years later, in 1993.

Since 1993 builders have added more than 4,000 miles (6,436 km) of new roads to the IHS. As the United States grows and changes, people will need to add even more roads. The existing roads will always need repairing. So this wonder of transportation will always be a work in progress.

"Virtually all major urban areas in the United States are connected to one another by the interstate highway network."

—*American Highway Users Alliance, 1996*

Interstate highways have no traffic lights or stop signs. Drivers get on and off the highways via ramps. Interchanges—where several highways come together—can be very complex, especially in big cities.

A GRAND ACHIEVEMENT

The IHS is good for the U.S. economy. IHS highways carry about 75 percent of all the products Americans buy—everything from fresh fish to computers to concrete. And think of all the gas stations, motels, and restaurants along IHS highways. These businesses give jobs to countless workers.

The IHS has been a lifesaver in emergencies. In September 2005, for example, motorists in southeastern Texas used the IHS to flee Hurricane Rita. Government officials ordered millions of people living along the Texas coast to evacuate, or leave their homes. To help them, traffic engineers turned all lanes on both sides of three interstate highways into outbound lanes. Even though the lanes were clogged with cars, twice as many vehicles could move north and west to escape the oncoming storm.

The IHS gives drivers freedom of movement. They can travel long distances quickly and safely. People who live in the suburbs can take the IHS to their jobs in the city. People who live in the city can drive to jobs in the suburbs.

By any standard, this wonder of transportation is a grand achievement. The IHS contains only a small fraction of the nation's roads. But it carries nearly half of all vehicle traffic. When drivers want to travel long distances quickly and safely, they use the IHS.

6 THE Queen Elizabeth 2

The Queen Elizabeth 2 *leaves a harbor in Australia on its way back to Great Britain.*

One hot, sunny morning, a carefree young woman went out for a walk. She liked the smell of the salt air from the nearby ocean. She sat awhile to watch a tennis match. Later, she passed by a beauty salon, a movie theater, and a computer center. Then she passed a department store. She thought about stopping in to shop, but too many other people had the same idea. Next came a tasty lunch at the Princess Grill. Then it was off to the pool to cool off before returning to her room.

The Queen Elizabeth 2 *was a floating city.*

> *"Enjoy QE2 while you can, for when she is gone, there won't be anything quite like her ever again."*
>
> — *Ben Lyons, travel writer, circa 2007*

This young woman's journey lasted about three hours. During that time, she walked nearly 3 miles (5 km). Crowds surrounded her the whole time, but she never set foot on a busy city street. She did her walking in the middle of the Atlantic Ocean. She took her walk among the twelve decks of a luxury cruise ship.

And this was not just any old cruise ship. It was the *Queen Elizabeth 2*, better known as the *QE2*. The *Queen Elizabeth 2* was named after the *Queen Elizabeth*, an earlier luxury liner. In its more than forty years at sea, from 1967 to 2008, the *QE2* took more than two million passengers on luxury cruises. It regularly cruised the North Atlantic Ocean. It carried passengers between Southampton, England, and New York City. Once a year, it took a round-the-world cruise.

LUXURY AND TRAGEDY

Not all sea voyages are luxurious. In earlier centuries, many immigrants took ships from Europe to America. Most passengers on immigrant ships did not have much fun. The areas where they slept and ate were often cramped, wet, and dirty.

The first luxury cruise ships appeared in the early 1900s. The most famous by far was the British ship *Titanic*. Its fame came from terrible tragedy. The White Star Line, the company that built *Titanic*, boasted that the ship was unsinkable. It proved to be anything but.

On its very first voyage, in 1912, *Titanic* hit an iceberg and sank. The ship did not carry enough lifeboats for everyone on board. By the time a rescue ship arrived, the icy waters had taken their deadly toll. *Titanic* carried 2,229 passengers and crew. Only 713 survived.

WAR AND AIRLINERS

The *Titanic* tragedy did not scare people away from luxury sea travel. During the 1920s and 1930s, rich and famous passengers filled luxury cruise ships.

Prices were high, but so were the ships' standards. Suites were roomy and richly furnished. Food and drink were of the highest quality. Guests dressed in fancy clothes to eat gourmet dinners. Musicians, singers, and actors entertained day and night. These ships were floating hotels designed mainly for the wealthy.

World War II changed ocean travel. During this conflict, warships threatened passenger ships. The seas became too dangerous for anyone but soldiers. Many shipping companies stopped running luxury cruises. Instead, they used their ships to carry soldiers.

After the war, luxury liners were back in business. But another obstacle soon appeared—this one in the sky. By the 1950s, people were flying across the Atlantic Ocean on passenger airplanes. Travel by air was less expensive and far speedier than travel by ship. When it came to choosing between the two, more and more wealthy people chose the air. People still took cruise ships. But they became a fun way to take a vacation rather than a luxurious way to cross the ocean.

The Cunard shipping line launched the *QE2* in 1967. During its first few years at sea, the *QE2* was known as the last of the true luxury liners.

Left: *Queen Elizabeth II, the queen of the United Kingdom, launches the* QE2 *in 1967. The first Queen Elizabeth reigned in the 1500s. Several ships have been named in her honor.* Right: *The QE2 takes off on its maiden voyage in 1967.*

The QE2 sails out of its home port of Southampton, England.

LAST OF THE LUXURY LINERS

The *QE2* is 963 feet (294 km) long. That's nearly as long as three football fields placed end to end. It weighs more than fifty-four thousand cars. It's taller than a seventeen-story building.

You might think such a big ship would be a slow mover. Not so. Before its retirement in 2008, the *QE2* was the fastest passenger liner on the seven seas. Its top speed was 32.5 knots. That's more than 37 miles (60 km) per hour. One passenger described his ride on the *QE2* as "a tremendous display of speed and power."

The *QE2* had room for 1,778 guests. A crew of 1,016 was on board to care for them. Among the crew were 107 cooks. They served about fourteen thousand meals each day.

The ship had machines that turned salty seawater into fresh drinking water. If anything went wrong with the ship's equipment, plumbers, electricians, and other skilled repair people stood ready to help. If anything went wrong with a passenger's health, medical doctors were always on board.

EVER *Wonder?*

What did people eat on luxury liners? The *Bremen* was a German liner from the 1930s. A typical lunch menu included no fewer than eighty separate items. Many dishes were made with rare and strange ingredients. Among the fish dishes were eel in wine jelly and anchovies with creamed lobster over cucumber slices. Among the meat dishes were lamb's tongue with rice, duckling with applesauce, and marrowbones with toast.

Seven Wonders of Transportation

At Your *Service*

Every guest on the *QE2* had a cabin steward. While guests were out, the stewards came in and tidied up. One guest wrote, "When you return from dinner, your bed will be turned down with chocolates and a copy of the next day's ship's newsletter. There will be one or two cute animals made of towels nearby."

As a luxury liner, the QE2 was known for its unparalleled service. Above: *A cabin steward cleans a room on the QE2.* Below: *An employee carries a tray down one of the many richly decorated hallways aboard the QE2.*

"We're spoiled to death, we get to see the whole world and meet the most incredible people."
—*Beatrice Muller, who lived on board the* QE2 *for several years, 2008*

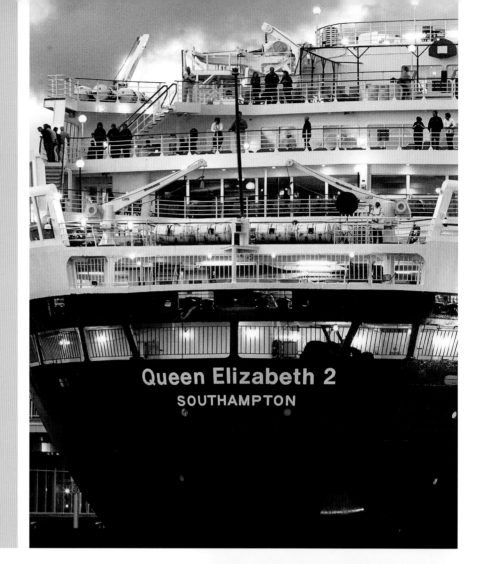

The twelve decks of the QE2 evolved during its more than forty years in service.

Queen Elizabeth 2
SOUTHAMPTON

ONE-CLASS CRUISING

When the ship first launched in 1967, the top decks were strictly private. They were for first-class passengers only. These passengers paid the most money and got the best cabins (rooms) and food. The largest cabin, a grand suite on the top deck, took up 900 square feet (84 sq. m). Moving downward, the cabins grew smaller and less expensive. The *QE2*'s smallest cabin was 73 square feet (6.8 sq. m). It was big enough to hold a bed, but not much else.

Over the years, the *QE2* changed. Cunard turned it from a luxury liner into a fun-for-all

TO THE MOON and *Back*

All told, the *QE2* sailed farther than any other ship. It logged more than 4.8 million miles (7.7 million km). How far is that? It's like traveling to the moon and back ten times.

cruise ship. Year by year, workers rebuilt the ship from top to bottom. When the ship first launched, only first-class passengers could use the top decks. By the time the *QE2* was ready to retire, all twelve decks were open to all passengers. But even with these changes, the *QE2* was still luxurious.

INTO RETIREMENT

In October 2008, the *QE2* made its last trip to the United States. It reached New York City on the morning of October 16. Admiring crowds cheered as the ship passed the Statue of Liberty. Twelve hours later, it sailed away into the twilight. It headed back to Great Britain.

In November 2008, the *QE2* made its final voyage. It sailed from Great Britain to Dubai, part of the United Arab Emirates in the Middle East. The government of Dubai paid the Cunard line about $100 million for the ship. Dubai plans to turn the ship into a new kind of wonder. It will become a luxury hotel. It will remain docked at a pier in Dubai. No one will ever sail on the *QE2* again.

The QE2 sails past the Statue of Liberty on its last voyage out of New York Harbor. The QE2 then made one final trip from Great Britain to Dubai before retiring from ocean travel.

7 Supergreen Cars

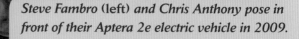

Steve Fambro (left) and Chris Anthony pose in front of their Aptera 2e electric vehicle in 2009.

STEVE FAMBRO LIKES DISCOVERING WHAT THINGS ARE MADE OF AND HOW TO MAKE THEM BETTER. HE USED TO WORK WITH ROBOTS. THAT WAS HIS DAY JOB. ON WEEKENDS HE WORKED IN HIS GARAGE. HE WRESTLED WITH A QUESTION: HOW COULD HE GET BETTER GAS MILEAGE OUT OF HIS FORD F150 PICKUP TRUCK?

A woman charges the battery in her electric car.

The truck was big and boxy. It did not let the wind flow easily around it. It drove like a big wall, pushing back against the wind, fighting it. And the truck was made of heavy metal. Its weight and boxy shape hurt gas mileage.

Fambro believed that he could do better. He decided to design his own car from the ground up. Together with his business partner, Chris Anthony, Fambro did just that. The result was the Aptera.

WHY GO SUPERGREEN?

The Aptera is a "supergreen" car. Supergreen cars are designed to run on a fuel source other than gasoline. What's wrong with gasoline? First, it comes from crude oil. There is only so much crude oil left inside Earth. When we run out, there will be no more gasoline to power cars.

But that is not the only problem with gasoline. Cars that run on gasoline damage the environment. Each year the average gasoline-powered car sends nearly 6 tons (5.4 metric tons) of greenhouse gases into the air. Greenhouses gases are not friendly to humans or animals. They pollute the air. Air pollution can make people sick with lung cancer, asthma, and other diseases.

Greenhouse gases are not friendly to Earth either. These gases trap the sun's heat, much like the glass roof on a greenhouse. They cause Earth's temperature to rise. This global warming is melting ice at the North Pole and the South Pole. The more the ice melts, the less ice there will be to cool Earth. Experts predict that melting ice will also cause sea levels to rise. Rising seas could flood islands and coastal regions around the world. And that's not all. Scientists agree that global warming could lead to more extreme weather, such as hurricanes, droughts, and floods.

BUT DOESN'T ELECTRICITY *Pollute?*

Electric cars get their electricity from power plants. To produce that electricity, most power plants burn coal. Burning coal is like burning gasoline. It pollutes the air with greenhouse gases. Even so, experts say that driving an electric car still cuts air pollution. Burning coal for electricity releases 70 percent less pollution than burning gasoline to run cars.

> *"There are two reasons why we must get out of oil. . . .*
> *One: it is running out. Two: we cannot afford to burn it."*
>
> —Jeremy Leggett, oil and solar energy expert, 2005

A STRANGE BEAST

Supergreen cars are a wonder of transportation because they present an Earth-friendly alternative to gasoline-powered vehicles, polluted air, and global warming. Some supergreen cars run on vegetable oil, solar (sun) energy, and other nonpolluting fuels. These cars are still in the experimental stage. You are not likely to see them on the road anytime soon.

Plug-in hybrids and all-electric cars are the most popular supergreen cars by far. More and more car companies are designing and building them. Plug-in hybrids run on a combination of electric power and gasoline. All-electric cars run on electric power only.

Fambro's company produces both plug-in hybrids and all-electric cars. Aptera plans to start selling these cars in late 2009 or early 2010. The cars have attracted a lot of attention.

*The Toyota Prius hybrid (right) **runs on both electricity and gasoline, but it is not a plug-in hybrid.***

The Aptera is a two-person car. It has seats in front for a driver and a passenger. The cargo area behind the seats can hold fifteen bags of groceries. Both Aptera models look alike. The first thing that stands out is the curvy, streamlined shape. The Aptera has no square corners. Its doors open upward, like wings. The car has three wheels instead of four. The front of the car has two wheels, and the back has one.

People make jokes about the Aptera's strange appearance. One writer called it "a cross between a dolphin and a helicopter." Others say it looks like something that just dropped in from outer space. People have compared it to a gigantic wasp, a strange beast, a teardrop, and a bee.

SLIPPERY AND STRONG

There are good reasons for this strange look. With an ordinary car, "sixty percent of the [engine's] energy goes to push the air out of the way," Fambro explains. That adds up to a lot of energy wasted. The Aptera, on the other hand, is aerodynamically designed. It slips and slides through the wind instead of fighting it. The Aptera looks strange because, in this case, strange equals streamlined.

The average gasoline-powered car weighs about 3,500 pounds (1,588 kg). The Aptera weighs less than half that, or about 1,700 pounds (771 kg). The car is lightweight, but it is also strong. According to its makers, the car can support the weight of two elephants.

A TRICYCLE *Car?*

People criticize the Aptera for different reasons. Some people don't like its looks. One journalist wrote, "Electric cars have gotta be the way of the future with their clean [pollution]-free engines . . . but are they all going to look as strange as the tricycle-wheeled Aptera?" Others have more practical complaints, such as this one: "What happens when you try to avoid a pothole? If the two front wheels straddle the pothole, you'll get quite a bump when the rear wheel falls in."

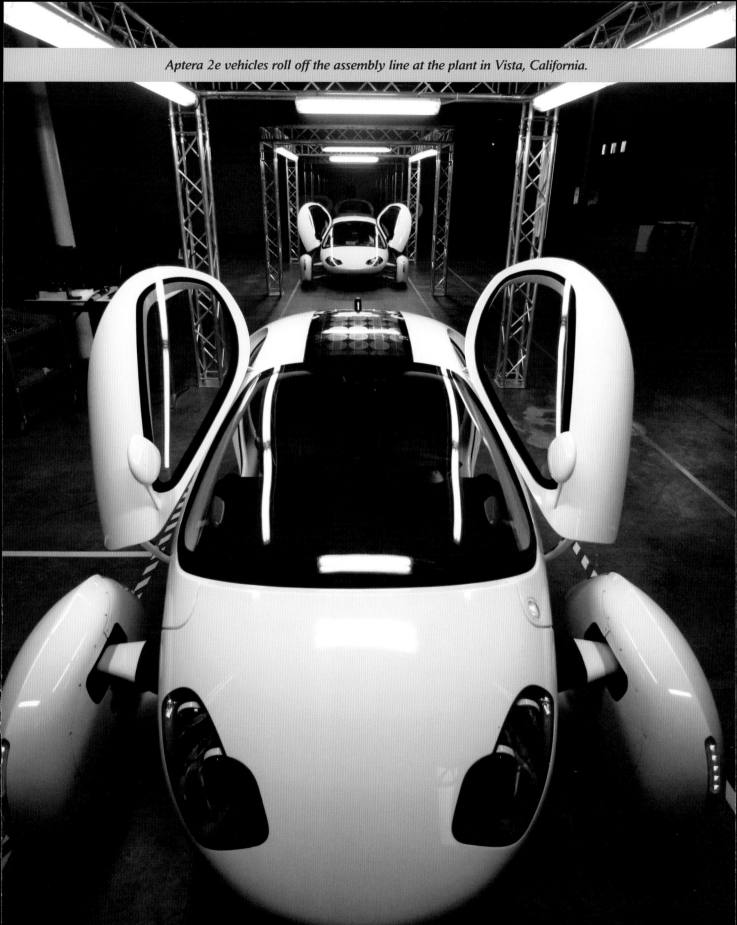
Aptera 2e vehicles roll off the assembly line at the plant in Vista, California.

POWER AND RANGE

In a typical car, a gasoline engine powers the wheels. In Aptera models, the power is electric. A battery powers an electric motor, which runs the front wheels. The all-electric model runs on battery power only. The plug-in hybrid model has a small gasoline-powered generator. The generator helps keep the battery charged while the car is moving.

When the battery runs low, the owner must recharge it by plugging it into a wall socket. Recharging the battery takes about eight hours. If the owner plugs the battery in at night, the car will be all powered up by morning.

In any electric car, range is crucial. Range is the distance the car can travel before the battery must be recharged. The Aptera plug-in hybrid has a range of about 600 miles (965 km). The all-electric Aptera has a smaller range, because there is no gas generator to help keep the battery charged. The all-electric's range is about 100 miles (161 km). For many drivers, that's enough. Most people use their cars mainly for driving to and from work and for running errands. They drive an average of 40 miles (64 km) a day, well within the range of an all-electric Aptera.

With electric vehicles, consumers will stop pumping gas (left) and start charging batteries (right).

DOLLARS AND *Minutes*

One man wrote to a magazine to explain why he intends to buy an Aptera. He was not thinking about the environment. His reasons involved money and time. He wrote, "I commute alone 55 miles [88 km] each day, round trip. The Aptera is perfect for me, [it] will cut my commute cost to $1.00 per day—if I took the bus, it would be $8.00 per day, by comparison, and take me 2 hours, versus 40 minutes in the Aptera. It's a no-brainer for me."

WILL THEY BUY ELECTRIC?

Aptera chief Paul Wilbur says, "We hope to change everyday driving forever." The company also announced, "We are committed to putting 100,000 Apteras on the road by 2015." But can these goals be met?

Electric cars are not a new idea. People built the first electric cars in the late 1800s. But these cars never caught on. Will they catch on in the 2000s? Switching to a supergreen car involves a big change. People are used to driving gasoline-powered cars. These cars have unlimited range. They don't need eight hours of recharging. Filling up at a gas station takes just a few minutes. Will people be willing to change their driving habits?

They might. After all, electricity costs only one to two cents per mile, versus ten to twenty cents per mile for gasoline. And electric cars don't send tons of polluting greenhouse gases into the air. About 600 million gasoline-powered vehicles travel the world's streets each day. If they were supergreen instead, Earth would be a cooler and cleaner planet.

"Twenty years from now, we'll look at cars that waste energy the way we look at litter today. They will make us feel weird."

—*Steve Fambro, 2008*

TIMELINE

ca. 3000 B.C.	People in the Middle East invent the wheel.
ca. 500 B.C.	Traders and travelers begin using the Silk Road between Asia and the Middle East.
102 B.C.	Chinese armies capture one thousand "heavenly horses" for Emperor Wu Ti.
A.D. 1274	Marco Polo first meets Chinese ruler Kublai Khan.
1298	*The Travels of Marco Polo* is published.
ca. 1350	Traders stop using the Silk Road as ocean travel becomes more common.
1863	The London Underground subway system opens.
1865	French author Jules Verne writes *From the Earth to the Moon*, the first novel to imagine a trip in a spaceship.
1885	Manufacturers sell the first modern-style bicycle, the Rover Safety Bicycle.
1892	The Wright brothers open the Wright Cycle Exchange in Dayton, Ohio.
1900	The Paris, France, subway system opens.
1903	The Wright brothers make the first piloted, powered airplane flights at Kitty Hawk, North Carolina.
1905	The London Underground switches from steam trains to electric trains.
1912	The luxury ocean liner *Titanic* sinks after hitting an iceberg.
1919	The First Transcontinental Motor Convoy travels across the United States to promote a national highway system.
1956	Workers complete the first section of the Interstate Highway System.
1967	The luxury cruise ship *Queen Elizabeth 2* takes to the seas.
1969	U.S. astronaut Neil Armstrong becomes the first person to walk on the moon.
1974	Chinese farmers discover terra cotta warriors while digging a well near the Silk Road city of Xi'an.
2005	Terrorists explode bombs on London's subways, killing fifty-four passengers and injuring hundreds.
2008	The *Queen Elizabeth 2* retires after sailing more than 4.8 million miles (7.7 million km).
2009	The Aptera car company begins selling supergreen cars.

CHOOSE AN EIGHTH WONDER

Now that you've read about the Seven Wonders of Transportation, do a little research to choose an eighth wonder. You may enjoy working with a friend.

To start your research, look at some of the websites and books listed on pages 75–77. Use the Internet and library books to look for more information. What other discoveries or inventions have been important in transportation? Think about inventions and discoveries that have
- *helped people move faster*
- *helped move a lot of people or cargo*
- *used new kinds of technology*

You might even try gathering photos and writing your own chapter on the eighth wonder.

8

GLOSSARY AND PRONUNCIATION GUIDE

aerodynamics (air-oh-dy-NA-mihks): the study of how air flows around a body moving through it

archaeologist (ahr-kee-AH-leh-jihst): a scientist who studies buildings, tools, and other remains of ancient civilizations

biomechanics (by-oh-meh-KA-nihks): the study of how living things move

biplane: an airplane that has two sets of wings, one above the other

caravan: a group of human travelers and pack animals on a long journey

convoy: a group of vehicles traveling together, often to provide one another with protection

excavate: to dig up objects that have been buried under the ground

friction: the rubbing of one body against another. Friction causes moving things to slow down.

generator: a machine that converts mechanical energy into electrical energy

global warming: an increase in Earth's average temperature. Many scientists think that greenhouse gases are causing global warming.

green: helpful to the environment

greenhouse gas: a gas such as carbon dioxide that traps the sun's heat near Earth

infrastructure (IHN-fruh-struk-shur): roads, highways, railroad tracks, bridges, and other systems that help communities work efficiently and safely

lift: an upward movement of air under an airplane's wings

Silk Road: a network of ancient trade routes connecting Asia and the Middle East

subway: an underground transportation system

technology: tools, techniques, and processes that people use to make life easier

transportation: the movement of people and things from one place to another

wind tunnel: a testing facility used to study how air moves around vehicles and other objects

SOURCE NOTES

10 Silkroad Foundation, "Han Emperor Wu-ti's Interest in Central Asia and Chang Chien's Expeditions," *Silkroad Foundation*, 2000, http://www.silk-road.com/artl/wuti.shtml (March 2, 2009).

12 Silkroad Foundation, "Marco Polo and His Travels," *Silkroad Foundation*, 2000, http://www.silk-road.com/artl/marcopolo.shtml (March 2, 2009).

12 Stefano Tronci, "The Land Where the East Becomes Far," *Expat Arts Magazine*, 2008, http://expatarts.wordpress.com/2008/11/23/the-land-where-the-east-becomes-far/ (March 2, 2009).

15 Xuanzang, "Xuanzang's Record of the Western Regions," *Silk Road Seattle*, 2003, http://depts.washington.edu/silkroad/texts/xuanzang.html (March 5, 2009).

19 Amir Moghaddass Esfehani, "The Bicycle's Long Way to China," *Imperial Tours*, 2004, http://www.imperialtours.net/bicycle.htm (March 5, 2009).

20 Wikiquote, "Cycling," *Wikiquote*, 2009, http://en.wikiquote.org/wiki/Cycling (May 5, 2009).

27 David L. Pike, "The Underground Railway in Victorian London," *Institute for Advanced Technologies in the Humanities*, 2006, http://www2.iath.virginia.edu/london/Archive/On-line-pubs/2001/paper5.html (March 2, 2009).

28 Ibid.

33 Edward Walford, "Underground London," *British History Online*, 2009, http://www.british-history.ac.uk/report.aspx?compid=45233 (May 1, 2009).

40 Wilbur Wright and Orville Wright, "O. & W. WRIGHT. FLYING MACHINE. Patent Application filed May 22, 1903," *To Fly Is Everything*, 2009, http://invention.psychology.msstate.edu/i/Wrights/WrightUSPatent/WrightPatent.html (March 2, 2009).

41 Smithsonian National Air and Space Museum, "Inventing a Flying Machine," *Smithsonian National Air and Space Museum*, 2009, http://www.nasm.si.edu/wrightbrothers/fly/1903/construction.cfm (March 10, 2009).

42 Wilbur Wright and Orville Wright, "O. & W. WRIGHT. FLYING MACHINE. Patent Application filed May 22, 1903."

42 Wikipedia, "Apollo 11," *Wikipedia*, 2009, http://en.wikipedia.org/wiki/Apollo_11 (March 2, 2009).

46 Logan Thomas Snyder, "President Dwight Eisenhower and America's Interstate Highway System," *HistoryNet.com*, 2008, http://www.historynet.com/president-dwight-eisenhower-and-americas-interstate-highway-system.htm (March 2, 2009).

48 Richard F. Weingroff, "The Lincoln Highway," *Federal Highway Administration*, 2009, http://www.fhwa.dot.gov/infrastructure/lincoln.cfm (March 6, 2009).

48 D. D. Eisenhower, "Infrastructure," *Federal Highway Administration*, 2009, http://www.fhwa.dot.gov/infrastructure/convoy.cfm (March 2, 2009).

51 Wendell Cox and Jean Love, "40 Years of the U.S. Interstate Highway System: An Analysis, the Best Investment a Nation Ever Made," *Public Purpose*, 2004 http://www.publicpurpose.com/freeway1.htm#econ (March 2, 2009).

56 Ben Lyons, "Letter from . . . a QE2 Devotee."

58 Ben Lyons, "Letter from . . . a QE2 Devotee," *Cruise Critic*, 2009, http://www.cruisecritic.com/articles.cfm?ID=495 (March 2, 2009).

59 Absolute Write Water Cooler, "Cruise Ship Cabins," *Absolute Write*, 2009, http://www.absolutewrite.com/forums/showthread.php?t=125900 (March 2, 2009).

59 BBC News, "The Woman Who Lives on the QE2," *BBC News*, 2009, http://news.bbc.co.uk/2/hi/uk_news/england/hampshire/7719605.stm (March 7, 2009).

65 Jeremy Leggett and David Jenkins, "When Will the Oil Run Out," *Prospect Magazine*, 2005, http://www.prospect-magazine.co.uk/article_details.php?id=7156 (March 10, 2009).

66 John Fuller, "How the Aptera Hybrid Works," *How Stuff Works*, 2009, http://auto.howstuffworks.com/aptera-hybrid.htm (May 25, 2009).

66 Eric Hagerman, "1 Gallon of Gas, 100 Miles—$10 Million: The Race to Build the Supergreen Car," *Wired*, 2007, http://www.wired.com/cars/futuretransport/magazine/16-01/ff_100mpg?currentPage=all (March 2, 2009).

66 Kit Eaton, "First Aptera Electric Cars Roll Out: Vehicle of the Future?" *Fast Company*, 2009, http://www.fastcompany.com/blog/kit-eaton/technomix/first-aptera-electric-cars-roll-out-vehicle-future (March 2, 2009).

66 Logan Ward, "Top 10 New World-Changing Innovations of the Year," *Popular Mechanics*, 2009, http://www.popularmechanics.com/science/research/4286850.html?page=2&series=60 (March 10, 2009).

69 Tony Borroz, "The Car of the Future Promised for October," *Autopia*, 2009, http://blog.wired.com/cars/2009/01/1st-pre-product.html (March 2, 2009).

69 Huliq News, "Aptera Focuses on Final Enhancements," *Huliq News*, 2008, http://www.huliq.com/1/73329/aptera-focuses-final-enhancements (March 2, 2009).

69 Helen Walters, "Driving the Aptera 2e," *Businessweek*, 2009, http://www.businessweek.com/innovate/next/archives/2009/02/driving_the_apt.html?chan=top+news_top+news+index+-+temp_innovation+%2Bamp%3B+design (March 2, 2009).

69 Logan Ward, "Top 10 New World-Changing Innovations of the Year," *Popular Mechanics*, 2009, http://www.popularmechanics.com/science/research/4286850.html?page=2&series=60 (March 10, 2009).

SELECTED BIBLIOGRAPHY

Cardwell, Donald. *Wheels, Clocks, and Rockets: A History of Technology*. New York: W. W. Norton and Company, 2001.

Davies, Peter. *American Road: The Story of an Epic Transcontinental Journey at the Dawn of the Motor Age*. New York: Henry Holt and Company, 2002.

Donzel, Catherine. *Luxury Liners: Life on Board*. New York: Vendome Press, 2006.

Duncan, Dayton, and Ken Burns. *Horatio's Drive*. New York: Alfred A. Knopf, 2003.

Gordon, Stewart. *When Asia Was the World*. Philadelphia: Da Capo Press, 2008.

Herlihy, David V. *Bicycle: The History*. New Haven, CT: Yale University Press, 2004.

Polo, Marco. *The Travels of Marco Polo*. Peter Harris, ed. New York: Everyman's Library, 2008.

Smith, Stephen. *Underground London: Travels beneath the City Streets*. Boston: Little Brown, 2005.

Sorensen, Eric. *Seven Wonders for a Cool Planet: Everyday Things to Help Solve Global Warming*. San Francisco: Sierra Club / Counterpoint, 2008.

Sperling, Daniel, and Deborah Gordon. *Two Billion Cars: Driving Toward Sustainability*. New York: Oxford University Press, 2009.

Thubron, Colin. *Shadow of the Silk Road*. New York: HarperCollins Publishers, 2007.

Tobin, James. *To Conquer the Air: The Wright Brothers and the Great Race for Flight*. Glencoe, IL: Free Press, 2004.

FURTHER READING AND WEBSITES

Books

Childress, Diana. *Marco Polo's Journey to China*. Minneapolis: Twenty-First Century Books, 2008. This book in the Pivotal Moments in History series reveals how Marco Polo's manuscript about traveling to China on a trade exhibition changed the world.

Doeden, Matt. *Green Energy: Crucial Gains or Economic Strains?* Minneapolis: Twenty-First Century Books, 2010. This book debates arguments for and against green energy, including comparing effectiveness of alternative energy sources versus cost.

Fridell, Ron. *Earth-Friendly Energy*. Minneapolis: Lerner Publications Company, 2009. This colorful book deals with global warming and the Earth-friendly energy sources used to combat it, including hydrogen fuel cells and biofuels.

Haduch, Bill. *Go Fly a Bike! The Ultimate Book about Bicycle Fun, Freedom and Science*. New York: Dutton Children's Books, 2004. This all-about-bikes book tells how bikes work, explains BMX stunts, and much more.

Herbst, Judith. *The History of Transportation*. Minneapolis: Lerner Publications Company, 2006. This book covers inventions that reshaped history, including the wheel, boats, the steam engine, the internal combustion engine, and air travel.

Macaulay, David. *Underground*. New York: Sandpiper, 1983. The author takes us down into a subway and shows and tells us what's there. The book includes an explanation of the cut-and-cover method used in the London Underground.

MacLeod, Elizabeth. *The Wright Brothers: A Flying Start*. Tonawanda, NY: Kids Can Press, 2009. This book covers the brothers' early experiments with gliders and includes historic photographs and documents.

McPherson, Samantha Sammartino and Joseph Sammartino Gardner. *Wilbur and Orville Wright: Taking Flight*. Minneapolis: Twenty-First Century Books, 2004. This biography of the Wrights details the years of research and failed designs before the brothers succeeded in taking flight.

Sutton, Richard, and Elizabeth Baquedano. *Car.* New York: Dorling Kindersley, 2005. Photographs and text together show how cars have changed and developed, from the earliest models to modern vehicles.

Weintraub, Aileen. *Mountain Biking*. New York: Children's Press, 2003. This book covers all aspects of the sport, with lots of colorful photographs.

Woods, Michael and Mary B. Woods. *Ancient Transportation: From Camels to Canals.* Minneapolis: Twenty-First Century Books, 2000. Find out how ancient engineers designed and built ships, bridges, and roads without the help of modern equipment in this book about ancient transportation.

Websites

Energy Kid's Page

http://www.eia.doe.gov/kids/

Designed especially for young people, this website features loads of information on energy and transportation. Timelines, lists of fun facts, and an energy glossary are included.

The National Highway System

http://www.fhwa.dot.gov/planning/nhs/

Want to see what the roads look like in your state? Go here for detailed highway maps of all fifty states.

StarChild: A Learning Center for Young Astronomers

http://starchild.gsfc.nasa.gov/docs/StarChild/StarChild.html

Learn about exploring the universe as an astronomer and astronaut at this website from the National Aeronautics and Space Administration.

Wayback: Flight

http://pbskids.org/wayback/flight/index.html

This Public Broadcasting Service site is all about the history of flight. It has special sections on the Wright brothers and other pioneers of aviation.

INDEX

ABOUT THE AUTHOR

Ron Fridell is a writer of news articles, short stories, textbooks, and more than thirty nonfiction books for young people. He has written about genetic engineering, forensic science, global warming, spying, Earth-friendly energy, world hunger, and terrorism. He lives in Tucson, Arizona, where he enjoys hiking and camping in the mountains.

PHOTO ACKNOWLEDGMENTS